"Freedom's greatest gift is the celebration of the individual."

America's Heart & Soul

by Louis Schwartzberg

A BlackLight Films Book

Design by Bruce Gordon

Printed in China

Library of Congress Cataloging-in-Publication Data on file.

"This is the story of Freedom, told one person at a time."

"America is not a melting pot,
it is a sizzling cauldron."

The heart and soul of America is a mixture of ideas and emotions that strengthen us and encourage us to persevere. It originates from the awe inspiring natural setting that we cherish, from the native peoples who established a reverence for the land, from the great leaders and thinkers who shaped a representative system that offers each of us a voice in shaping an entire nation, and from the personal stories of so many men and women who passionately struggle, sacrifice, laugh, innovate and endure whatever it takes to realize and celebrate freedom.

In the motion picture and in the book *America's Heart and Soul* Louis Schwartzberg presents a series of portraits broad enough to help us see and treasure this concept, one that we all recognize, and yet that is too difficult for most of us to put into words. He's captured something beautiful and very powerful, like the nation itself. And he's given us all a great gift; a reason to pause, reflect and to quietly celebrate our differences, to embrace them as an inspiration.

Robert Redford

"We are a free people, free to succeed or fail."

"We've invented this system of Democracy that people from all over the world can get together and can create something really truly wonderful if they work together and maintain their focus on a spiritual mission. And that's what America is about."

Robert Kennedy, Jr., Environmentalist
Democratic National Convention, Los Angeles, California

"The future belongs to those who are free to believe in their dreams."

"The thing I cherish most in my life is my freedom, and that was probably the reason
I quit the alcohol. To have more freedom."

"You get a horse that trusts you and you have a wonderful thing.
A life-long relationship that isn't gonna let you down and go away some time."

Thomas "Roudy" Roudebush, Horse Wrangler
Telluride, Colorado

"There's so many rules. God, I'd have less rules. We've experienced being free and unfettered human beings here, because there aren't many people and there isn't much government. Cherish your freedom."

Thomas "Roudy" Roudebush, Horse Wrangler
Telluride, Colorado

"Gospel came from slaves. While pulling their cotton sacks.
They'd moan…mmmm, nobody could stop them."

Mosie Burks, Gospel Singer
Jackson, Mississippi

"It's not just one kind of food or one kind of music or one kind of landscape.
It's the wonderful diversity of this country that makes this place so great."

Marc Savoy, Accordion Maker
Eunice, Louisiana

"A man come to me one time and he said, 'How do you know you're a mountain person?'
I said, 'Well, cut me open right here. You won't see a heart, what you'll see is a mountain range.
Mist hanging in the hills. That's my heart.'"

"This is where I learn to listen. Most people pray and they're doing the talking. When I weave I must listen."

Minnie Yancey, Rug Weaver
Berea, Kentucky

"What has made this nation great?
Not its heroes, but its households."

"There is nothing more important than watching your children grow up. Learn new things every day."

"The thing about working seven days a week is you don't have to worry about going back to work on Monday when Sunday comes. Don't dread it, you know."

George Woodard, Jr., Dairy Farmer
Waterbury, Vermont

"I realized that the many one room schools up these hollows had no books at all, except text books, and some of those were well worn, indeed. I always wanted to put good books in children's hands. I supposed I had a kind of sense of mission. This was a place I felt I could make a difference."

James Still, Appalachian Writer
Berea, Kentucky

"Well, it's very important for me to teach children because I want to keep the heritage alive and pass it on from generation to generation."

Johnnie Billington, Blues Musician
Lambert, Mississippi

"Here in this land of opportunity where
Success and failure rest side by side
Big ol' roads run coast to coast
Lots to see if you can catch a ride."

John Mellencamp
"The World Don't Bother Me Now"
Original Theme Song for "America's Heart and Soul"

"Beauty is also to be found in a day's work."

"My theory has always been let the wood speak for itself. And I don't think that we as individuals can improve much on what Mother Nature has done with a piece of wood."

"I always keep my pieces open vessels so that
you can see the beauty of the wood inside,
as well as the beauty of the wood on the outside."

Rude Osolnik
Berea, Kentucky

"A handmade hat is much better than a mass produced hat because it's like maintaining an art. I think making hats is just my way of speaking to the world."

Alexander Conley III, Hatmaker
Seattle, Washington

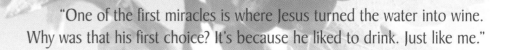

"One of the first miracles is where Jesus turned the water into wine.
Why was that his first choice? It's because he liked to drink. Just like me."

Ed Holt, Wine Maker
Santa Maria, California

"Catching lobsters, teaching kids. Both things, you've got to persevere. Not catching lobsters...better set your traps a little differently. Same thing with kids...rig up your lessons in a different way. You know, put a little different bait in there. You eventually catch lobsters, and you can eventually teach the kids."

June Kantz Pemberton, Lobsterman and Teacher
Matinicus, Maine

"We had a little explosion on a rig one time, and I burned my old head a little bit. A few years later, I started working for a company that put fires out instead of being on a rig where they started."

Ace Barnes, Oil Well Firefighter
Red River, New Mexico

BOOTS &c COOTS
OIL WELL FIRE FIGHTERS
AND BLOWOUT SPECIALISTS

"Every time I go on a job, my little one worries about me. My partner who was killed in an explosion was like a second father to him. But he's seen me go and he's seen me come back. So he knows Daddy will always come back."

James Tuppin, Oil Well Firefighter
Bridgeport, Texas

"Coal is a polluting resource, but it's also a resource that put the beans on the table all my life."

Jim Faley, Coal Miner
Pikesville, Kentucky

"My Grandfather was a Coal Miner, my Dad was a Coal Miner, and I'm a Coal Miner. It's all I know how to do, and all I want to do."

Greg Durmott, Coal Miner
Pikesville, Kentucky

"You have a great business when the goal of the business is to meet the need, to create the product. You make money as a by-product of meeting a need and doing a great job of it."

Ben Cohen, cofounder, Ben & Jerry's Ice Cream
Williston, Vermont

"If the steel mill goes down, this town will be dead.
I don't know what the answer is…but I know it's not quitting."

James Andreozzi, Steel Worker
Weirton, West Virginia

"The sad part about all this is our steel mills and our steel workers in this country are the most efficient and the most environmentally friendly in the world. But yet it's our jobs being taken away…and that's hard to swallow."

James Andreozzi, Steel Worker
Weirton, West Virginia

"My dream is just to be successful enough where I can bring home
a gold record and give it to my Mother and my Father.
Just pretend that I was in music college for ten years."

Frank Pino, Rock Musician
Waltham, Massachusetts

"Yac's a good guy, in the basic Brooklyn-Queens
meaning of the word, he's a Goodfella.
You know, he's always got your back in a fight.
He's the crown king of New York City Messengers."

Mike Dee, Bike Messenger
New York, New York

"This land is your land, this land is my land."

Woodie Guthrie

"The real death of America will come when everyone is alike."

"I think the difference between a boys' and a girls' league
is the girls don't focus on winning or losing.
They're just out there having a great time."

Mike Cullinan, Coach, Pawtucket Slaterettes
Pawtucket, Rhode Island

"Young people nowadays, they don't raise a garden, they don't raise chickens.
Young wives, they don't know how to gut a chicken. They're too lazy to do it.
They just want big fun and the big money."

Shelby Manual, Owner, Feed Store
Eunice, Louisiana

"Laughing. It works universally for everybody, and it's the best therapy in the world. If you're laughing, you're probably happy."

"This wacky stuff comes from a real hot shower in the morning beating against my bald spot."

Paul Stone, Explosive Artist
Creede, Colorado

"I wish I had a dime for every smile. I'd be wealthy."

Larry Fuentes, Car Artist
San Francisco, California

"I've been working on this car for six years now. It's old and tired. Realistically and financially, I just can't do it anymore. And I decided to crush it myself. I get to give it its own death. I get to put it to sleep. It's going to be the perfect ending."

Cheri "Rat Girl" Brugman, Car Artist
San Francisco, California

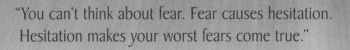

"You can't think about fear. Fear causes hesitation.
Hesitation makes your worst fears come true."

Biker Sherlock, Street Luger
San Diego, California

"Freedom lives in the soul
and keeps the passion alive."

"In my opinion, the people are the stars. Without them, I would be nobody."

Little Milton, Blues Musician
Las Vegas, Nevada

"If you can let yourself be taken in by the music without thinking it's just so loud, or it's just so different. Then you can experience something that is such a gift to the world."

Danielle de Niese, Opera Singer
New York, New York

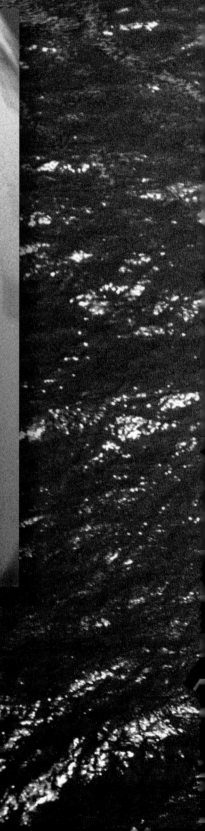

"I always felt like I was a leaf floating in the wind, even though it's the most freedom you can ever have, it's also the most structured. Because in aerobatic flying, one mistake could be your last."

Patty Wagstaff, Aerobatic Pilot
St. Augustine, Florida

"I don't like standing on a cliff.
Soon as I'm anchored, I'm free."

Amelia Rudolph,
Founder, Bandaloop Cliff Dancers
Muir Beach, California

"One piece sparks my imagination. Then I go out and fall in love with several other pieces to combine it with. To me, it isn't junk. It's rusty gold."

Dan Klennart, Junk Artist
Elbe, Washington

"Trombone Shorty is my little brother and I help him be responsible for himself through music. The most important thing in my life is passing the music on to the children, that's how I overcome adversity."

James Andrews and Trombone Shorty, Jazz Musicians
New Orleans, Louisiana

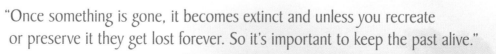

"Once something is gone, it becomes extinct and unless you recreate
or preserve it they get lost forever. So it's important to keep the past alive."

Kenwood Cassens, Pilot
Rhinebeck, New York

"We're at the oldest Eastern European Jewish synagogue in America.
When I'm here, I feel like I'm back playing for my ancestors."

David Krakauer, Klezmer Clarinetist
New York, New York

"I came from Europe when I was 17 to follow my dreams.
You know people always dream of coming to America
and seeing what it's really like with their own eyes."

David "Chase" Peirsman, Mural Artist
Los Angeles, California

"You can put tomatoes, onions, cilantro, anything that you want in Salsa.
So it's the same. You just dance and put your heart into it."

Luis Vazquez, Salsa Dancer
Long Beach, California

"In unity there is strength."

"I think just because women are boxers, that doesn't mean we're not feminine. I think strong women are a beautiful thing."

Marsha Valley, Boxer
Los Angeles, California

"He treat me like I'm special. He work with me, play with me. And he like a Father to me."

Frederick Nelson, Young Boxer
Chicago, Illinois

"I'm trying to give back. Trying not to allow the streets to swallow them up. Because as long as he stays in here, he's safe."

Michael Bennet, Olympic Boxer
Chicago, Illinois

"Lots of veterans have come to live here in Alaska, because of the freedom that we have. The ability to drive down the street with a shotgun in our Easy Rider rifle rack."

Geoffrey Nelson, Vietnam Veteran
Bamboo Bar, Haines, Alaska

"I want to see your eyes opening up with not the shades or shadows covering them, but love beaming with light from your eyes, which tells me it's coming from your soul. I want that. Heart and Soul."

Reverend Cecil Williams, Glide Memorial Church
San Francisco, California

"You want people that don't bite their tongue, when you're trying to take care of your life."

Terry Harper, Glide Memorial Church
San Francisco, California

"It's a good job, and it's keeping me from being in the soup line, 'cause I've been on that side.
I had a slight gap in my employment history, between 1968 and 1995."

Mickey Haggedy, Glide Memorial Church
San Francisco, California

"I hope the wind don't get my hat.
It probably wouldn't hit the ground until Nebraska."

Francis Daellenbach, Wyoming Rancher
Cheyenne, Wyoming

"Dreams are the touchstones of our character."

"Being a blind mountain climber is like being a Jamaican bobsledder. The words don't necessarily go together.
For me, all the great things that have ever come to me, have come through reaching out,
and I think life is just a process of reaching out into the darkness."

Erik Weihenmayer, Blind Climber
Golden, Colorado

"Every kid's dream in Little League is to play the major leagues.
They're searching for that one perfect swing, where it comes off the bat and you never feel it."

Andy Burress, Minor League Baseball Player, Mudville 9
Sacramento, California

"Just play. Have fun. Enjoy the game."

Michael Jordan

"The Boston Marathon is my favorite race. The people along the way are the best.
They have such enthusiasm that when my Dad and I run by, the adrenaline rush is unbelievable."

"I wouldn't be running today if Rick didn't ask me to."

Dick and Rick Hoyt, Father and Son Triathletes
Boston, Massachusetts

"I feel that Rick is the athlete and I'm just out there loaning him my arms and my legs so that he's able to compete like everybody else. I am the body, Rick is the heart, and mobility is freedom."

Dick and Rick Hoyt, Father and Son Triathletes
Boston, Massachusetts

"Freedom is never more than one generation away from extinction."

Ronald Reagan
President of the United States

"I was talking to a woman that lost a son and she said something that I just want to share with you this morning. She said when you lose your parents, you lose your past. When you lose a spouse, you lose the present. But when you lose your children, you lose your future."

Heather Lende, Disc Jockey
Haines, Alaska

"We're just common folks. We're firefighters."

Emergency Company 10
Seattle, Washington

"My father is an eagle, my mother is a raven.
And that is why an eagle is so dear to me."

Charles Jimmie, Sr., Tlingit Elder
Klukwan, Alaska

"When you finally get a chance to see an eagle fly again, it gets a second chance. When they leave us, they go with our spirit. And they take it with them to our ancestors above."

Charles Jimmie, Sr., Tlingit Elder
Klukwan, Alaska

"To live free or die is not just an empty slogan on the license plate."

John Harrigan, Newspaper Editor
Colebrook, New Hampshire

To Tell The Stories
Behind the Scenes of America's Heart & Soul

Mother nature has been my best teacher. I've learned so much from shooting beautiful images of nature: composition, texture, patience and most importantly the passion and art of chasing the light. And once I had begun to master the technique of shooting the magic moments of nature, the next big challenge was to capture the spirit of people and their stories, and letting the light enhance and dramatize the emotion of the moment.

The circular relationship between people and the land is a theme that has always intrigued me. I think that people shape the land, and the land shapes the people's psyche. So when I started working on this project back in the mid 1980s, I tried to find people whose work or art is intrinsic to the locale.

When I present these stories, the landscape, the lighting and the environment are all critical to the production. Together these elements give each story its own flavor, and that helps me to understand why people do what they do and how their lives reflect their particular region of the country.

I graduated from UCLA where I started off as a history major. During all the political and social unrest of the early 70s I used my camera to document the protests and the confrontations on campus. I realized that doing a photo essay was much more relevant and interesting than writing a thesis, so that turned me on to photography. From fine art photography I was exposed to experimental filmmaking. And once I saw the giant screen I knew that was the canvas where I wanted to work.

ABOVE: *Filmmaker Louis Schwartzberg in Williston, Vermont.*

RIGHT: *Every time we did helicopter work we tried to take it to the edge, to get the most dramatic shots. Safety is always the top priority, but if you don't push it to the edge, just up to the point of being unsafe, rarely is it an exciting or spectacular shot.*

SPACECAM

"AMERICA"

ROLL	SCENE	TAKE
S 3		SERIES
C 3		

Director L. SCHWARTZBERG

Camera L. SCHWARTZBERG

6. 01   MOS DAY EXT

ABOVE: *A little film trickery... For the shot where explosion artist Paul Stone shoots a bowling ball out of a cannon directly into the camera lens, we actually placed a mirror in front of the cannon, then aimed the camera into the mirror. The camera and crew survived, but sadly, the mirror did not.*

RIGHT: *Filming Erik Weihenmayer ice climbing in Quray, Colorado. In order to get the most dramatic shots, we needed to be close, and shoot straight down. We rigged ropes across the ravine with a harness and pulley system so that we could float the camera just above his head looking down. For added dramatic effect we shot with ultra wide lenses, but suspended from a rope it is difficult to get your own feet out of the shot. As you pull your feet back and lean forward you risk flipping over and having the camera slip off your shoulder.*

I became very interested in a seldom-used technique called time-lapse cinematography. This technique called for the camera to shoot a frame of film every few seconds or few minutes, compared with shooting 24 frames each second, which is what's required for smooth real-time motion. I started shooting time-lapse nature photography. With time-lapse we could see something that took a couple of hours to unfold in the natural world, like a flower opening or a bank of storm clouds rolling across the sky, in a smooth ten-second scene. I loved the sense of wonder of shooting time-lapse clouds, fog covering a valley, city lights coming on in the evening, and whatever else might capture my imagination. I always shot with 35mm motion picture film, because I appreciated the highest quality that this large negative made possible. But 35mm is expensive, so I kept my costs down by shooting time-lapse. I invested a lot of my time without shooting very much film. Perhaps this process helped me realize that the most precious commodity is time.

Little by little, people started hearing about this eccentric guy shooting all sorts of time-lapse subjects. Initially I did some work for the Cousteau Society, and a lot of my early work was used in the feature film *The Secret Life of Plants*, and *Koyaanisqatsi*. This led to a variety of work including music videos and special effects for features like *Altered States*, *The Heavenly Kid* and *The Karate Kid*, as well as high-end television production. During the years when I was directing commercials and doing a lot of image campaigns for network television, I noticed the inner cities go through an evolution of rebirth. Young people were moving back into the cities, row houses were being fixed up, and whole neighborhoods were being brought back to life. It was inspiring for me to see cities that had once seemed bound for decay and were now being rejuvenated and revitalized.

That got me thinking about creating a different kind of documentary; one that wove stories of people together with the land and cities where they lived. Finding these stories turned out to be quite a challenge, and the project took a lot longer to do than I ever expected. When I started back in the early 90s, it's hard to imagine, but the Internet wasn't available. Back then, to research story possibilities I would call up local newspapers and television stations since they were the ones who always had the pulse of the community.

I also read a lot of newspapers. I still feel that every time I pick up a newspaper I'm able to find an angle on a story. And obviously the Internet was eventually very helpful in researching the stories as well.

If a story inspired me, it would get added to my growing file. Over the years some of the teenage stories grew-up, and some of the old people passed away. But I had a core group of stories that I kept developing. And then it was time to start filming. One of the most important lessons I learned was to keep myself open to the opportunity for serendipity to occur. Serendipity (or sometimes mistakenly referred to as luck) doesn't happen without being prepared. If I had my crew out on the road and some interesting situation or person crossed my path, I'd think it was fate, and we would do our best to turn those stories into gold. The process was a combination of research, being prepared, and allowing opportunity to strike.

When I would approach people about doing a story about them, I would ask them, "Would you be in my film? It's an independent project and I have hopes and aspirations that someday this might be on the big screen. That's my dream but the truth is I'm out here on my own time and my own nickel. I'd love to tell your story and my job is to make you look good." I think that made them comfortable to open up and trust me. They knew I wasn't going to throw them some weird curve ball. I was only going to ask them about their passion and their expertise. Most of us love to talk about what we do and what we know best, especially our art, our passions or our work. The people I filmed enjoyed the whole production process.

During filming, I taught my crew to be low key and as unobtrusive as possible, since all of our film equipment— cameras, dollies, cables, lighting and grip equipment—made us look like Martians to some of the people we were shooting. And natural curiosity sometimes became a serious distraction to my mission. These folks were curious about all my stuff, and of course my crew was curious about their stuff. I had to impose a pretty strict discipline to keep the story focused. It was so easy to get off track when the crew started asking the storyteller questions, because the storyteller was so darn interesting.

ABOVE: *To get that feeling of vertigo when filming the Bandaloop dancers we mounted a crane with a remote head so that we could reach out over the cliff and shoot straight down. The hardest part was carrying the crane in sections up the rocky cliffs, with all the lead counter weights, and breaking it apart and hauling it back down in the twilight.*

With natural light as my guide I'd approach the production of a story based on where the light was going to be. This immediately told me how to structure each day. The most magical shots came from being in the right place at the right time with the camera ready to shoot. If the light was going to be beautiful shining on the barn in the morning, then we'd start shooing outside the barn. Then, when the harsh midday light approached we'd go inside. At sunset we'd make sure the cameras were loaded and ready at the right spot to capture the low angle warm light. Working this way I quickly adopted a process where I could sort through all the options, and give my crew an outline that became the production schedule for the day. It worked out pretty well. As producer, director, and cinematographer there were no ego clashes in the meetings of my mind.

ABOVE: *A filmmaker's greatest asset is being inventive and doing whatever it takes to get the shot. Like opening the side of a minivan and shooting out the door, or doing a lot of handheld filming with bungee cords. The coolest shots of the bike messenger were made by mounting the camera on his handlebars and letting him ride between cars in traffic.*

RIGHT: *When we shot the steel mill in Pennsylvania, it was freezing cold outside, and just as cold inside. When a big bar of molten steel would pass by, it felt great to finally get warmed up. But you had to be careful — I always want to get close ups with wide-angle lenses, and I was standing on a grate in the floor when I noticed there was smoke coming off the bottom of my boots. Before we were finished shooting, the heat from the steel had melted my lens hood.*

THIS PAGE: *When we mounted our cameras on the wing tip and in the cockpit of Patty Wagstaff's aerobatic stunt plane, she told us she was going to be going more than 100 miles an hour and pulling eight g's in her turns and dives. Soon you're thinking, "Wow, I hope this is going to work!" With the help of Patty's mechanic, we fastened the cameras down the best we could. But when she hit the maximum g-force, the film magazine actually snapped off the camera and flew past her head. We also had a video camera in the cockpit, and video playback shows the magazine sailing through the cockpit, with the film spooling right past her head. After that, we gaffer taped the magazine to the body so it could handle the force, and all went well.*

RIGHT: *I wanted to do a story about the fact that more than 50 percent of Los Angeles residents are Hispanic. I thought, wouldn't it be great to do a story about salsa dancing — it's visual, exciting and local. We discovered that L.A. is the salsa capital of the world as far as having the most inventive dancing. It's a place where people come from all over the world to mix their talents and styles.*

FAR RIGHT, TOP: *The crew poses for the camera, as Louis continues to chase the light.*

FAR RIGHT, BOTTOM: *Louis in action.*

RIGHT: *One of the most dangerous situations occurred when I was shooting Roudy Roudebush, the cowboy. I was on horseback and had the camera handheld on my shoulder. I'm not really a horseback rider, but they told me not to worry because this was a mellow horse and there wouldn't be a problem. So there I was, with one hand on the camera and one hand on the saddle. A roll of 35mm film is only four minutes in length, so I ran out of film before we finished shooting the scene. Each roll of film is a quick-release "magazine" which is very convenient — unless it doesn't engage perfectly with the camera, in which case it makes a sound that's like a coffee grinder. And, of course, that's exactly what happened. The camera made this terrible noise, just inches behind the horse's ears. For a split second the horse was calm, then all of a sudden he bolted. So now I'm holding the film magazine in one hand and the camera in the other. My thighs are gripping for my life around the body of the horse as he runs full out. After about ten seconds (which seemed like forever) Roudy galloped up and grabbed the reins and calmed the horse down. Roudy started yelling in my face, "Why didn't you drop that camera and grab the saddle! You could have broken your neck!" Well, first off, a cameraman's inborn instinct is to never drop the camera. The other thing Roudy probably didn't realize is that a camera like this costs $140,000 — and it was my camera. It's the only one I ever purchased new in my entire life and I was just starting to make payments on it. You just don't drop a camera, especially when it's yours.*

During production, we ended up shooting almost 100 stories. When it finally came time to move into the editing room the final selection process became very difficult—there was only room for 28 of those stories in the completed movie. The stories which were not selected, weren't weaker; they just didn't fit the mosaic of the film as well as the others.

My parents instilled in me an appreciation and love for the ideals of America. They were both holocaust survivors, and I know they came to this country with nothing. But through hard work they were able to create opportunity for themselves and for their children. And even though as we grow up we learn that it isn't always a level playing field for all people, the truth is that compared to any other country, there is more freedom and opportunity here than anywhere else.

It's important that people continue to strive to make the social reality come closer to the highest ideals of freedom and democracy. Thomas Jefferson inscribed those ideals in the Declaration of Independence, but it was far from perfect back then. And it's not perfect now, but it keeps getting better. It's an evolving process. The hope and the goal is for every generation to continue the struggle for freedom, or risk losing it.

When people watch *America's Heart & Soul* or read this book, I hope they hear the call to "find their passion." If you find your passion, I think you'll be happy, it will rejuvenate your soul, and you can still make a living.

One of the great things about making a documentary like America's Heart & Soul is to let it be a voyage of discovery, not to force it into a pre-conceived notion of what it's supposed to be. To always be in a state of readiness for the light to strike, like the unexposed film.

If I learned one thing from traveling across this country and speaking to people, it's that people want to maintain their own culture. They don't want it to be watered down and homogenized by the mass media or conglomerates. We want to keep our different heritage, our varied music and food. We appreciate work that involves our hands, our minds, and our hearts. And we appreciate quality, if given the choice. Diversity, freedom, passion, eccentricity, and tolerance make us a strong and great country.

Acknowledgements

I would first like to thank my family for all that they have taught me. My wife Jan and daughters Lara and Jessica who kept me grounded and helped me maintain a sense of humor. My Dad for igniting the love of photography as he changed the bathroom into a darkroom in the humid run-down tenement apartments of Brooklyn. While he set up his photo enlarger, in the dark I witnessed the magical alchemy as a four-year old holding onto his boxer shorts in the dark. My Mom has been my greatest inspiration. Although she survived years in Auschwitz, she emerged with a powerful love of life that was contagious and taught me to never give up. This is why stories of people who have overcome adversity and have a passion for life are so dear to me.

My greatest teacher has been Mother Nature. She taught me composition, beauty, patience and hooked me on "chasing the light." Once I learned to master the craft she offered me another challenge, capturing magical moments with people and having the light intensify the emotion.

That set me on a voyage of discovery that led to the creation of this book and the motion picture, *America's Heart and Soul.* I would like to thank Jake Eberts, whose heart, integrity, and passion brought this project to Disney. I am indebted to Dick Cook who had the courage and determination to champion the project and share the vision. I would like to thank Lylle Breier whose boundless energy rallied all the folks at Disney in helping this project find an audience. Sincere thanks to my friends at Kodak for supporting documentary filmmakers. Bruce Gordon's artistic book design brought the imagery to another level. Last but not least, my hard core unit at BlackLight Films: Vincent Ueber, Rob Sherman, Sarina Volman, Kylee Kennedy, J.C. Earle, Brian Funck, Tom McGah, Chris Mohr, Grady Candler and Richie Pechner, who help me produce, shoot, and edit all the imagery.

Cherish your Freedom.